This diary is from a series of personal journals that are **meant to be found**. I know what you're thinking, "But doesn't that defeat the purpose?" And to that I'd say "Sure, but let's look at reality..."

In the event that it IS found, wouldn't you have something to say to the finder? Why have a picture of a kitten on the cover that only you will ever see? Won't you get sick of that kitten? I mean, I might not but that's beside the point. You might. And more than anything, it would be nice to greet the person who found it with a specific message. As I write this, I can think of about 50 potential messages that folks might want to send to their diary finder / stalker/ spying friend/ mother/ spouse / kids. That's the thing, you just never know who it's going to be, or when it's going to happen. But it's probably going to happen.

Published by Luckiest Girl Publishing
(tweet your journal-in-real-life pic &
Follow us on Facebook)
Printed by Amazon
(reach out to them if the print job is bad)
Designed by Lisa Russell
(who is more of a writer/coach than a designer)
Written by YOU!

Enjoy

Hot tip about indexing:

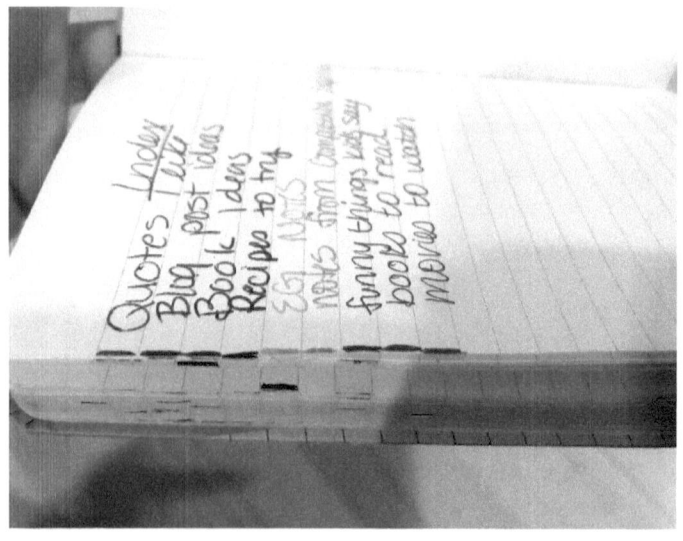

Sometimes you want to keep track of specific things.

Use the last page as an index

Each line is like a tab that's labeled in the index

Mark each page to match your index page

So easy
Super handy

www.ingramcontent.com/pod-product-compliance
Lightning Source LLC
Chambersburg PA
CBHW020447220526
45464CB00002B/894